A Pocket Book
of Prayers

for Busy People

christian
art gifts

Contents

The Lord's Prayer

Our Father in heaven,
hallowed be your name,
your kingdom come,
your will be done on earth
as it is in heaven.
Give us today our daily bread.
Forgive us our debts,
as we also have
forgiven our debtors.
And lead us not
into temptation,
but deliver us
from the evil one.
Matthew 6:9-13

Stillness
and
Serenity

Let Me Listen to the Quiet

Let me listen to the quiet
to the hallowed voice of God,
not rising up to follow
till my inner feet are shod
in accordance with the Guidebook
for my ways – His precious Word,
shutting out all other voices
that would clamor to be heard.
Let me listen in the quiet
while His loving hand outpours
all I need, He goes before me
opening – and closing – doors!

∽ Alice Hansche Mortenson ∽

Serenity Prayer

God grant me the serenity to
accept the things I cannot change,
the courage to change the things I can,
and the wisdom to know the difference.
Living one day at a time;
enjoying one moment at a time;
accepting hardship
as a pathway to peace.
Taking, as He did, this sinful world
as it is, not as I would have it;
trusting that He
will make all things right
if I surrender to His will;
that I may be reasonably happy
in this life
and supremely happy with Him
forever in the next.

Reinhold Niebuhr

Still Dews of Quietness

Drop Thy still dews of quietness,
Till all our strivings cease:
Take from our souls the strain and stress;
And let our ordered lives confess
The beauty of Thy peace.
Breathe through the pulses of desire
Thy coolness and Thy balm;
Let sense be dumb, its beats expire:
Speak through the earthquake,
wind and fire,
O still small voice of calm!

John Greenleaf Whittier

Teach Us to Wait

Teach us,
O Father, stillness and confident peace
in Thy perfect will,
Deep calm of soul, and content
in what Thou wilt do with these lives
Thou hast given.
Teach us to wait and be still,
to rest in Thyself,
to hush this clamorous anxiety,
to lay in Thine arms
all this wealth Thou hast given.
Thou lovest the souls that we love
with a love as far surpassing our own
as the glory of noon
surpasses the gleam of a candle.
Therefore will we be still,
and trust in Thee.

— J. S. Hoyland —

The Whisper of His Voice

Father,
Who hast told us to listen to Thy voice,
give us ears to hear Thy lightest whisper.
The daily work
and the rush of life around us,
and the clamor of our own fears
and self concern,
make such a noise
that it is difficult to be quiet before Thee,
and so we lose the sound of Thy voice.
Teach us how to be more still.
Teach us how to shut our doors
around us to all other thoughts,
and to make a deep silence in our hearts.
Then speak to us,
and we shall be strong to hear,
strong to do, strong to follow Thee utterly.
Through Jesus Christ our Lord.
Amen

Prayers of Health and Healing

A Quiet Place

'Mid all the traffic of the ways,
Turmoils without, within,
Make in my heart a quiet place,
And come and dwell therein:
A little shrine of quietness
All sacred to Thyself,
Where Thou shalt all my soul possess,
And I may find myself:
A little shelter from life's stress,
Where I may lay me prone,
And bare my soul in loneliness,
And know as I am known:
A little place of mystic grace,
Of self and sin swept bare,
Where I may look upon Thy face,
And talk with Thee in prayer.

∾ *John Oxenham* ∾

Guidance
and Knowing
God's Will

As God Wills

O Lord, Thou knowest what is best for us; let this or that be done, as Thou shalt please. Give what Thou wilt, and how much Thou wilt and when Thou wilt. Deal with me as Thou thinkest good. Set me where Thou wilt, and deal with me in all things just as Thou wilt. Behold, I am Thy servant, prepared for all things: for I desire not to live unto myself, but unto Thee; and, oh, that I would do it worthily and perfectly!

Thomas à Kempis

Prayer of Abandonment

Father,
I abandon myself into Your hands;
do with me what You will.
Whatever You may do I thank You:
I am ready for all, I accept all.
Let only Your will be done in me,
and in all Your creatures.
I wish nothing more than this, O Lord.
Into Your hands I commend my soul:
I offer it to You
with all the love of my heart,
for I do love You, Lord,
and so I need to give myself,
to surrender myself into Your hands,
without reserve,
and with boundless confidence,
because You are my Father.
Amen

⤳ Charles de Foucauld ⤳

Face the Day with Peace

O Lord, grant me to greet the coming day in peace. Help me in all things to rely upon Thy holy will. In every hour of the day reveal Thy will to me. Bless my dealings with all those who surround me. Teach me to treat all that comes to me throughout the day with peace of soul, and with the firm conviction that Thy will governs all. In all my deeds and words guide my thoughts and feelings. In unforeseen events let me not forget that all are sent by Thee. Teach me to act firmly and wisely, without embittering and embarrassing others. Give me strength to bear the fatigue of the coming day with all that it shall bring. Direct my will, teach me to pray, pray Thou Thyself in me.
Amen

Metropolitan Philaret of Moscow
(19th century)

The Right Path

Dear God,
Help me to take the right path in life and
help me to know right from wrong.
Show me a way to get through life and its
problems,
no matter how hard they are.
Help me to build a life I can be proud of
and
show me the way to make a happy life.
I put my trust in You as You are a God
who loves us no matter who we are.

⬥ Craig Adams ⬥

Spiritual Growth

For this reason, since the day we heard
about you, we have not stopped praying
for you and asking God to fill you with
the knowledge of his will through all
spiritual wisdom and understanding.
And we pray this in order that you may
live a life worthy of the Lord and may
please him in every way: bearing fruit
in every good work, growing in the
knowledge of God, being strengthened
with all power according to his glorious
might so that you may have great
endurance and patience, and joyfully
giving thanks to the Father, who has
qualified you to share in the inheritance
of the saints in the kingdom of light.

Colossians 1:9-12

A Godly Vision

Give us, O God,
the vision which can see
Thy love in the world
in spite of human failure.
Give us the faith
to trust Thy goodness
in spite of our ignorance and weakness.
Give us the knowledge
that we may continue to pray
with understanding hearts,
and show us what each one of us
can do to set forward
the coming day of peace.

Frank Borman

For Guidance to Do His Will

My Lord God, I have no idea where I am going. I do not see the road ahead of me. I cannot know for certain where it will end. Nor do I really know myself, and the fact that I think that I am following Your will does not mean that I am actually doing so. But I believe that the desire to please You does in fact please You. And I hope I have that desire in all that I am doing. I hope that I will never do anything apart from that desire. And I know that if I do this You will lead me by the right road though I may know nothing about it. Therefore I will trust You always though I may seem to be lost and in the shadow of death. I will not fear, for You are ever with me, and You will never leave me to face my perils alone.

⤙ Thomas Merton ⤚

Open the Eyes of Our Heart

I keep asking that the God of our Lord
Jesus Christ, the glorious Father, may
give you the Spirit of wisdom and
revelation, so that you may know him
better.

I pray also that the eyes of your heart
may be enlightened in order that you
may know the hope to which he has
called you, the riches of his glorious
inheritance in the saints, and his
incomparably great power for us who
believe.

Ephesians 1:17-20

Surrender to God's Will

Lord,
I give up all my own plans and purposes,
all my own desires and hopes
and accept Thy will for my life.
I give myself, my life, my all,
utterly to Thee to be Thine forever.
Fill me and seal me with Thy Holy Spirit,
use me as Thou wilt,
work out Thy whole will in my life
at any cost now and forever.

~ Betty Stam ~

Solomon's Prayer for Wisdom

You have shown great kindness to your servant, my father David, because he was faithful to you and righteous and upright in heart. You have continued this great kindness to him and have given him a son to sit on his throne this very day. Now, O LORD my God, you have made your servant king in place of my father David. But I am only a little child and do not know how to carry out my duties. Your servant is here among the people you have chosen, a great people, too numerous to count or number. So give your servant a discerning heart to govern your people and to distinguish between right and wrong. For who is able to govern this great people of yours?

1 Kings 3:6-9

God's Plans Fulfilled

O Living Spirit,
all our powers reclaim;
Let Thy compassion
set our souls aflame.
Form Thou in us
a purpose true and pure,
that what we build
together may endure.
High on the mountain
of Thy holiness
above the fogs,
where Thou canst own and bless,
help us the City of our God to build
where all Thy plans
for us may be fulfilled.

Henry Robins

Refuge in the Lord

In you, O LORD, I have taken refuge; let me never be put to shame. Rescue me and deliver me in your righteousness; turn your ear to me and save me.

Be my rock of refuge, to which I can always go; give the command to save me, for you are my rock and my fortress. Deliver me, O my God, from the hand of the wicked, from the grasp of evil and cruel men.

For you have been my hope, O Sovereign Lord, my confidence since my youth. From birth I have relied on you; you brought me forth from my mother's womb. I will ever praise you. My mouth is filled with your praise, declaring your splendor all day long.

⌒Psalm 71:1-6, 8 ⌒

Confession
and
Repentance

Going it Alone

Lord, I need others.
The way of man is too hard
to be trodden alone.
But I avoid the hands
outstretched to help me,
I want to act alone,
I want to fight alone,
I want to succeed alone.
And yet beside me walks a friend,
a spouse, a brother,
a neighbor, a fellow-worker.
You have placed them near me, Lord,
and too often I ignore them.
And yet it is together that we shall
overcome the world.
Lord, grant, that I may see, that I may
accept, all the Simons on my road.

Michel Quoist

For Grace

O Lord our heavenly Father,
Almighty and everlasting God,
who hast safely brought us
to the beginning of this day:
Defend us in the same
with Thy mighty power;
and grant that this day
we fall into no sin,
neither run into any kind of danger;
but that all our doings
may be ordered by Thy governance,
to do always what is righteous
in Thy sight;
through Jesus Christ our Lord.
Amen

The Book of Common Prayer

A Prayer for Forgiveness

Almighty Father, teach me to do everything with the utmost sincerity. Save me from posing even to myself. Make my life unaffected, simple and sincere. Cleanse me from selfishness; let my gaze be outward rather than inward. Teach me to think more of others than of myself. Forbid that my own interests should be paramount.

Pardon, I beseech Thee, all that is and has been wrong in my life and character. Had I always sought Thy will I should now have been strong in the Lord, instead of being the weak, slothful, vacillating creature that I am. But it is never too late. Help me to remedy the evil and henceforth to build with honesty and prayer.

Amen

∽ Walter James ∽

Cleanse Our Hearts

Almighty God,
unto whom all hearts be open,
all desires known,
and from whom no secrets are hid,
cleanse the thoughts of our hearts
by the inspiration of the Holy Spirit,
that we may perfectly love Thee
and worthily magnify Thy holy name.
Through Christ our Lord.
Amen

⤳ The Book of Common Prayer ⤳

A Confession

If my soul has turned perversely
to the dark;
If I have left some brother
wounded by the way;
If I have preferred my aims to Thine;
If I have been impatient
and would not wait;
If I have marred the pattern
drawn out for my life;
If I have cost tears to those I love;
If my heart has murmured
against Thy will,
O Lord, forgive me.

＞ *F. B. Meyer* ＞

For Freedom
Through His Love

Thy love to me, O God,
Not mine, O Lord to Thee,
Can rid me of this dark unrest,
And set my spirit free.
Thy grace alone, O God,
To me can pardon speak;
Thy power alone, O Son of God,
can this sore bondage break.
I bless the Christ of God,
I rest on love divine,
And with unfaltering lip and heart,
I call this Savior mine.

Horatius Bonar

A Cry for Mercy

Forgive me, my Father. When things have gone well with me I have left Thee out, crowded my days with work and pleasure and forgotten Thee. I have been so foolishly proud that I have imagined I could get on without Thee, so I have lost the sense of Thy dear presence from my life. I was content with human companionship and often scamped or omitted my prayers. Joy and health, success and comfort, youth and high spirits made me indifferent to Thee, who didst give them all. Let me in future see Thee in all Thy gifts, seek communion with Thee when I feel no need of Thee, and cling to Thee as I do to a human friend. Take Thy rightful place again, O Lord, for in Thee alone is life and enduring peace.
Amen

⸺ *Leslie Weatherhead* ⸺

Purify Our Thoughts

Almighty God,
unto whom all hearts be open,
all desires known,
and from whom no secrets are hid:
cleanse the thoughts of our hearts
by the inspiration of Thy Holy Spirit,
that we may perfectly love Thee,
and worthily magnify Thy holy name;
through Jesus Christ our Lord.

Unknown

Praise
and
Thanksgiving

Praise the Lord

Praise the LORD, O my soul;
    all my inmost being, praise
        his holy name.
Praise the LORD, O my soul,
    and forget not all his
        benefits –
who forgives all your sins
    and heals all your diseases,
who redeems your life from
        the pit
    and crowns you with love
        and compassion,
who satisfies your desires with
        good things
    so that your youth is renewed
        like the eagle's.

Psalm 103:1-5

God's Great Love

I call on you, O God, for you
will answer me;
give ear to me and hear my
prayer.
Show the wonder of your great
love,
you who save by your right
hand
those who take refuge in you
from their foes.
Keep me as the apple of your
eye;
hide me in the shadow of
your wings
from the wicked who assail me,
from my mortal enemies who
surround me.

Psalm 17:6-9

Exalt the Lord

Blessed be your glorious name,
and may it be exalted
above all blessing and praise.
You alone are the LORD.
You made the heavens,
even the highest heavens,
and all their starry host,
the earth and all that is on it,
the seas and all that is in them.
You give life to everything,
and the multitudes
of heaven worship you.

Nehemiah 9:5-6

A Song of Praise

My heart rejoices in the LORD; in the LORD my horn is lifted high. My mouth boasts over my enemies, for I delight in your deliverance. There is no one holy like the LORD; there is no one besides you; there is no Rock like our God. He raises the poor from the dust and lifts the needy from the ash heap; he seats them with princes and has them inherit a throne of honor. For the foundations of the earth are the LORD's; upon them he has set the world. He will guard the feet of his saints.

~1 Samuel 2:1-2, 8-9 ~

Praise to My God

How many are your works, O LORD!
In wisdom you made them all;
the earth is full of your creatures.
These all look to you to give them
their food at the proper time.
When you give it to them,
they gather it up;
when you open your hand,
they are satisfied with good things.
May the glory of the LORD
endure forever;
may the LORD rejoice in his works –
I will sing to the LORD all my life;
I will sing praise to my God
as long as I live.

Psalm 104:24, 27-28, 31, 33

Glory to the Lord

Glory to our ascended Lord
that He is with us always.
Glory to the Word of God,
going forth with His armies
conquering and to conquer.
Glory to Him who has led
captivity captive and given gifts
for the perfecting of His saints.
Glory to Him who has gone before
to prepare a place
in His Father's home for us.
Glory to the Author and the Finisher
of our faith; that God in all things
may be glorified through Jesus Christ,
to whom be all worship and praise,
dominion and glory;
now and forever and ever.
Amen

Sursum Corda

In the Midst of Busyness

I turn my thoughts quietly, O God,
away from self to Thee.
I adore Thee. I praise Thee. I thank Thee.
I here turn from this feverish life
to think of Thy holiness –
Thy love – Thy serenity – Thy joy –
Thy mighty purposefulness –
Thy wisdom – Thy beauty – Thy truth –
Thy final omnipotence.
Slowly I murmur these great words
about Thee and let their feeling
and significance sink into the deep places
of my mind and heart.

⌒ Leslie Weatherhead ⌒

To Live with the Lord

How simple for me to live with You, O
Lord. How easy for me to believe in You!
When my mind parts on bewilderment or
falters, when the most intelligent people
see no further than this day's end and do
not know what must be done tomorrow,
You grant me the serene certitude that
You exist and that You will take care
that not all the paths of good be closed.
Atop the ridge of earthly fame, I look
back in wonder at the path which I alone
could never have found, a wondrous
path through despair to this point from
which I too could transmit to mankind a
reflection of Your rays. And as much as I
must still reflect You will give me.

Alexander Solzhenitsyn

49

Honor God

Eternal God,
Father of all men,
cleanse and strengthen,
we beseech Thee,
the life we live this day;
that the work of our hands
and the thoughts of our hearts
may be acceptable in Thy sight,
and our lives may do honor
to Thy holy name;
through Christ our Lord.

Unknown

Lead Me in the Way Everlasting

Search me, O God, search me
and know my heart,
try me and prove me in the hidden part;
Cleanse me and make me
holy as Thou art,
and lead me in the way everlasting.
Give me the heart
that naught can change or chill,
the love that loves unchanged
through good or ill,
the joy that through
all trials triumphs still,
and lead me in the way everlasting.
Take my poor heart and only let me love
the things that always
shall abiding prove;
Bind all my heart-strings
to the world above,
and lead me in the way everlasting.

A. B. Simpson

Consecrating
Our Work
to God

Wait on Him

At Thy dear feet, once pierced for me
With cruel nails upon the tree,
I lay my life for use by Thee;
Henceforth to know no anxious care.
With cheerful heart my load to bear,
My sole resort – believing prayer.
No worry, lest my work be stayed;
No hurry, lest I be delayed,
By haste – to prayerlessness betrayed;
Not careful to be praised of man,
But only to be taught Thy plan –
What Thou wilt have me do, I can.

No need of gain, for Thou hast said
That if the beasts and birds are fed,
Thy children shall not lack for bread.
How sweet to live alone in Thee,
In danger to Thy wings to flee,
The name of Jesus all my plea!
Before Thee let Thy servant stand,
To watch Thine eye, Thy beckoning hand,
And promptly move at Thy command.
So shall my life be one sweet day,
Lifted up by heaven's cloudless ray,
A walk with God, a radiant way!

≺ A. T. Pierson ≻

Sanctified to Him

Oh, empty us of self,
the world and sin,
and then in all Thy fullness enter in;
Take full possession, Lord,
and let each thought
into obedience unto Thee be brought;
Thine is the power,
and Thine the will, that we
be wholly sanctified, O Lord, to Thee.

           ⌁ *C. E. J.* ⌁

Time

Lord, I have time,
I have plenty of time,
all the time that You give me,
the years of my life,
the days of my years,
the hours of my days,
they are all mine.
Mine to fill, quietly, calmly,
but to fill completely, up to the brim,
to offer them to You,
that out of their insipid water
You may make a rich wine
as You once made in Cana of Galilee.
I am not asking You tonight, Lord,
for time to do this and then that,
but Your grace to do conscientiously, in
the time that You give me,
what You want me to do.

Michel Quoist

Morning Prayer

We give thanks unto Thee,
heavenly Father,
through Jesus Christ Thy dear Son,
that Thou hast protected us
through the night
from all danger and harm;
and we beseech Thee to preserve
and keep us, this day also,
from all sin and evil;
that in all our thoughts, words, and deeds,
we may serve and please Thee.
Into Thy hands we commend
our bodies and souls,
and all that is ours.
Let Thy holy angel have charge
concerning us that the wicked one
have no power over us.
Amen

Martin Luther

For Great Endeavors

O Lord God,
when Thou givest to Thy servants
to endeavor any great matter,
grant us to know
that it is not the beginning,
but the continuing
of the same unto the end,
until it be thoroughly finished,
which yieldeth the true glory:
through Him who for
the finishing of Thy work
laid down His life,
our Redeemer, Jesus Christ.
Amen

Francis Drake

Trust in the LORD
with all your heart
and lean not
on you own understanding;
in all your ways
acknowledge him
and he will make
your paths straight.

Proverbs 3:5-6

To Please Him

With what shall I come before the LORD
and bow down before the exalted God?
Shall I come before him with burnt
offerings, with calves a year old? Will the
LORD be pleased with thousands of rams,
with ten thousand rivers of oil? Shall I
offer my firstborn for my transgression,
the fruit of my body for the sin of my
soul? He has showed you, O man, what is
good. And what does the LORD require of
you? To act justly and to love mercy and
to walk humbly with your God.

Micah 6:6-8

Yielding to God

O Great and Unsearchable God,
who knowest my heart,
and triest all my ways;
with a humble dependence
upon the support of Thy Holy Spirit,
I yield myself up to Thee,
as Thy own reasonable sacrifice,
I return to Thee Thy own.

Charles Spurgeon

Christ, Our Example

O Lord Jesus Christ, who didst hallow the workshop at Nazareth by Thy labor, and didst choose for Thy disciples men of the fields and of the sea and of the counting-house: grant to all who maintain the fabric of the world by their labor both integrity in their work and charity toward one another, that our common life may do honor to Thy name.

Bless, we beseech Thee, O Lord, all members of the professions, that they may pursue their several callings with learning, devotion, and skill; and grant that all thinkers and writers, musicians and craftsmen, being taught by Thy Holy Spirit, may enrich our common life with things that are true and lovely, and thus glorify Thy name; through Jesus Christ our Lord.

Unknown

Consecration

Use me, my Savior,
for whatever purpose
and in whatever way You may require.
Here is my poor heart,
an empty vessel:
fill it with Your grace.
Here is my sinful and troubled soul;
quicken it and freshen it
with Your love.
Take my heart for Your abode;
my mouth to spread abroad
the glory of Your name;
my love and all my powers
for the advancement
of Your believing people,
and never allow the steadfastness
and confidence of my faith to abate.

⤳ Dwight L. Moody ⤳

Partnership with God

Lord God and Father, I call upon Thee to enter all the avenues of my life today and to share every detail of it with me. Even as Thou hast called me to share with Thee Thy life, and all the wonders of it. As I am entering Thy treasures, Thou must now come in to possess all mine. As I am to share the destiny, glory, and future affairs of Thy Son, so would I now have Him share this small destiny of earth which is mine, the joys of it, and all its small matters – that we should be One, Thou and I, even as we are in Christ.

⤳ Jim Eliot ⤳

Filled with His Spirit

Into my heart, empty and waiting,
Over my soul, needy and still,
Through my whole being, consuming
and purging,
Sweep Thou, until –
Thou shalt see through my eyes,
Think through my brain,
Love through my heart,
And speak through my lips.
All of my being merging in Thine,
Holy Spirit divine.
Now filled with the source of all beauty
and power
Renewed life is mine,
Flowing within me each day and hour
From the Divine.

⤳ Miriam Reed ⤳

Consecration of
Talents to the Lord

You take the pen
and the lines dance.
You take the flute
and the notes shimmer.
You take the brush
and the colors sing.
So all things have meaning and beauty
in that space beyond time where You are.
How, then, can I hold back
anything from You?

— Dag Hammarskjöld —

To Reflect the Master

O God, help me all through today to do nothing to worry those who love me, to do nothing to let down those who trust me, to do nothing to fail those who employ me, to do nothing to fail those who are close to me.

Help me all through this day to do nothing which would be a cause of temptation to someone else or which would make it easier for someone else to go wrong; not to discourage anyone who is doing his best; not to dampen anyone's enthusiasm or to increase anyone's doubts.

Let me all through this day be a comfort to the sad, be a friend to the lonely, be an encouragement to the dispirited, be a help to those who are up against it. So grant that others may see in me something of the reflection of the Master whose I am and whom I seek to serve.

Amen

William Barclay

Joy in Work

Almighty God, who givest men wisdom
to devise and skill to complete all kinds
of work: give to all who labor with hand
and brain the help of Thy grace; that,
seeking the best in their craft, they may
find joy in their work; through Jesus
Christ our Lord.

O God, the Creator of all things, who
hast made men in Thine own image, so
that he must ever seek his joy in creative
work: have mercy, we beseech Thee,
on all who are unemployed, or whose
work is dull; and help us so to order our
common life that every man may have
work to do and find joy in doing it, to the
good of this nation and to the glory of
Thy name; through Jesus Christ our Lord.

Unknown

A Higher Life

O dear Savior,
be not impatient with us –
educate us for a higher life,
and let that life begin here.
May we be always in the school,
always disciples,
and when we are out in the world
may we be trying to put into practice
what we have learned at Jesus' feet.
What He tells us in the darkness
may we proclaim in the light,
and what He whispers in our ear
in the closets
may we sound forth
upon the housetops.
◦ Charles Spurgeon ◦

When
Things
Get Busy

A Tranquil Spirit

Guide me, O Lord,
in all the changes and varieties
of the world;
that in all things that shall happen,
I may have an evenness
and tranquility of spirit;
that my soul may be wholly resigned
to Thy divinest will and pleasure,
never murmuring
at Thy gentle chastisement
and fatherly correction.

⤳ *Jeremy Taylor* ⤳

When Feeling Weary

O Lord,
who art as the Shadow of a Great Rock
in a weary land,
who beholdest Thy weak creatures
weary of labor,
weary of pleasure,
weary of hope deferred,
weary of self;
in Thine abundant compassion,
and unutterable tenderness,
bring us, I pray Thee,
unto Thy rest.

Christina Rossetti

A Heart at Peace

Grant to me above all things
that can be desired,
to rest in Thee,
and in Thee to have my heart at peace.
Thou art the true peace of the heart,
Thou its only rest;
out of Thee all things
are hard and restless.
In this very pace,
that is, in Thee,
the One Chiefest Eternal Good,
I will sleep and rest.
Amen

⤳ Thomas à Kempis ⤳

Psalm 91

He who dwells in the shelter of the Most High will rest in the shadow of the Almighty. I will say of the LORD, "He is my refuge and my fortress, my God, in whom I trust."

If you make the Most High your dwelling – even the LORD, who is my refuge – then no harm will befall you, no disaster will come near your tent. For he will command his angels concerning you to guard you in all your ways; they will lift you up in their hands, so that you will not strike your foot against a stone. You will tread upon the lion and the cobra; you will trample the great lion and the serpent.

Psalm 91:1-2, 9-13

Many **Duties**

If this day
I should get lost
amid the perplexities of life
and the rush of many duties,
do Thou search me out,
gracious Lord,
and bring me back
into the quiet of Thy presence.

◦ *F. B. Meyer* ◦

The Courage to Simplify

Forbid it, Lord, that our roots become too firmly attached to this earth, that we should fall in love with things. Help us to understand that the pilgrimage of this life is but an introduction, a preface, a training school for what is to come. Then we see all of life in its true perspective. Then shall we not fall in love with the things of time, but come to love the things that endure. Then shall we be saved from the tyranny of possessions which we have no leisure to enjoy, of property whose care becomes a burden. Give us, we pray, the courage to simplify our lives.

⊱ Peter Marshall ⊰

Setting
Right
Priorities

Shine His Light

Stay with me, and then I shall begin to
shine as Thou shinest: so to shine as to be
a light to others. The light, O Jesus, will
be all from Thee. None of it will be mine.
No merit to me. It will be Thou who
shinest through me upon others. O let me
thus praise Thee, in the way which Thou
dost love best, by shining on all those
around me. Give light to them as well
as to me; light them with me, through
me. Teach me to show forth Thy praise,
Thy truth, Thy will. Make me preach
Thee without preaching – not by words,
but by my example and by the catching
force, the sympathetic influence, of what
I do – by my visible resemblances to Thy
saints, and the evident fullness of the love
which my heart bears to Thee.

John Henry Newman

A Busy Day

O Lord!
Thou knowest how busy
I must be this day:
If I forget Thee,
do not Thou forget me.

Jacob Astley

In the Morning

O God, our Father, deliver us this day from all that would keep us from serving Thee and from serving our fellowmen as we ought.

Deliver us from all coldness of heart; and grant that neither our hand nor our heart may ever remain shut to the appeal of someone's need.

Deliver us from all weakness of will; from the indecision which cannot make up its mind; from the inability to say No to the tempting voices which come to us from inside and from outside.

Deliver us from all failure in endeavor; from being too easily discouraged; from giving up and giving in too soon; from allowing any task to defeat us, because it is too difficult.

Grant unto us this day the love which is generous in help; the determination which is steadfast in decision; the perseverance which is enduring unto the end; through Jesus Christ our Lord.

William Barclay

Strength of Love

I pray that out of his glorious riches he may strengthen you with power through his Spirit in your inner being, so that Christ may dwell in your hearts through faith. And I pray that you, being rooted and established in love, may have power, together with all the saints, to grasp how wide and long and high and deep is the love of Christ, and to know this love that surpasses knowledge – that you may be filled to the measure of all the fullness of God.

Ephesians 3:16-19

Trust in God

Be merciful to me, O God, for
   men hotly pursue me;
all day long they press
   their attack.
My slanderers pursue me
   all day long;
many are attacking me in
   their pride.
When I am afraid,
   I will trust in you.
In God, whose word I praise,
   in God I trust; I will
   not be afraid.
What can mortal man
   do to me?

⌁ Psalm 56:1-4 ⌁

For Constant Improvement

We must praise Your goodness
that You have left nothing undone
to draw us to Yourself.
But one thing we ask of You, our God,
not to cease to work
in our improvement.
Let us tend toward You,
no matter by what means,
and be fruitful in good works,
for the sake of Jesus Christ our Lord.

⌒ Ludwig van Beethoven ⌒

The Fruit of the Spirit

O Lord,
reassure me with Your quickening Spirit;
without You I can do nothing.
Mortify in me all ambition,
vanity, vainglory, worldliness, pride,
selfishness, and resistance from God,
and fill me with love, peace,
and all the fruits of the Spirit.
O Lord, I know not what I am,
but to You I flee for refuge.
I would surrender myself to You,
trusting Your precious promises
and against hope believing in hope.
You are the same yesterday, today,
and forever; and, therefore,
waiting on the Lord,
I trust that I shall
at length renew my strength.
— William Wilberforce

An Eternal Perspective

O eternal God, though Thou art not such as I can see with my eyes or touch with my hands, yet grant me this day a clear conviction of Thy reality and power. Let me not go forth to my work believing only in the world of sense and time, but give me grace to understand that the world I cannot see or touch is the most real world of all. My life today will be lived in time, but eternal issues will be concerned in it. My business will be with things material, but behind them let me be aware of things spiritual.

O God, who dwellest in light unapproachable, yet also lives within me, give me grace today to recognize the stirrings of Thy Spirit within my soul and to listen most attentively to all that Thou hast to say to me. Let not the noises of the world ever so confuse me that I cannot hear Thee speak.

John Baille

Sensitivity to Others

O Lord, grant that each one who has to do with me today may be the happier for it. Let it be given me each hour what I shall say, and grant me the wisdom of a loving heart that I may say the right thing rightly.

Help me to enter into the mind of everyone who talks with me, and keep me alive to the feelings of each one present. Give me a quick eye for little kindnesses, that I may be ready in doing them and gracious in receiving them. Give me quick perception of the feelings and needs of others, and make me eager-hearted in helping them.

H. M. Soulsby

Take it Slowly

I will not hurry through this day.
Lord, I will listen by the way,
To humming bees and singing birds,
To speaking trees and friendly words;
And for the moments in between
Seek glimpses of Thy great unseen.
I will not hurry through this day;
I will take time to think and pray;
I will look up into the sky,
Where fleecy clouds and swallows fly;
And somewhere in the day, maybe
I will catch whispers, Lord, from Thee.

Ralph Spalding Cushman

Never Too Busy

O God, grant that all through today I may never find any request for help a nuisance. Let me never find a child a nuisance when he wants me to help him with his lessons or play with him in his games.

Help me never to find a nuisance anyone who asks me to show her how to do things, to assist her in her work, to listen to her troubles.

Grant, O God, that I may neither be too immersed in work or too fond of my own pleasure, that I may never be too busy and never too tired to help those who need help, even if they are the kind of people who get on my nerves or whom I instinctively dislike.

Help me to help, not only when it's pleasant to help, but when help is difficult and when I don't want to give it – through Jesus Christ my Lord.

Amen

William Barclay

Restless Spirits

Jesus, Thou joy of loving hearts,
Thou fount of life, Thou light of men,
From the best bliss that earth imparts
    We turn unfilled to Thee again.
Our restless spirits yearn for Thee,
Where'er our changeful lot is cast –
Glad when Thy gracious smile we see,
Blest when our faith can hold Thee fast.
    O Jesus, ever with us stay;
Make all our moments calm and bright;
Chase the dark night of sin away,
Shed o'er the world Thy holy light.

Bernard of Clairvaux

Longing for God

As the deer pants for streams of water, so my soul pants for you, O God. My soul thirsts for God, for the living God. When can I go and meet with God? My tears have been my food day and night, while men say to me all day long, "Where is your God?"

These things I remember as I pour out my soul: how I used to go with the multitude, leading the procession to the house of God, with shouts of joy and thanksgiving among the festive throng. Why are you downcast, O my soul? Why so disturbed within me? Put your hope in God, for I will yet praise him, my Savior and my God.

Psalm 42:1-6

For Moral Renewal

Father in heaven,
at a time when cynicism
and distrust are epidemic,
send us spiritual and moral renewal,
and let it begin with leadership.
Humble us, Lord, before it is too late.
Restore us to the dream
of our forefathers,
and forbid that we should be willing
to settle for anything less.

Richard Halverson

Joy in Simple Things

O God, who hast made the heavens and the earth and all that is good and lovely therein, and hast shewn us, through Jesus Christ our Lord, that the secret of joy is a heart freed from selfish desires: help us to find delight in simple things, and ever to rejoice in the richness of Thy bounty; through Jesus Christ our Lord.

Unknown

Strength
to Complete
the Task

The Way of the Lord

Teach me your way, O LORD,
    and I will walk in your truth;
give me an undivided heart,
    that I may fear your name.
I will praise you, O Lord my
       God, with all my heart;
I will glorify your name
      forever.
For great is your love
      toward me;
you have delivered me from
      the depths of the grave.

∾ Psalm 86:11-13 ∾

When Things go Wrong

Answer me quickly, O LORD; my spirit
fails. Do not hide your face from me or I
will be like those who go down to the pit.
Let the morning bring me word of your
unfailing love, for I have put my trust in
you. Show me the way I should go, for
to you I lift up my soul. Rescue me from
my enemies, O LORD, for I hide myself in
you. Teach me to do your will, for you
are my God; may your good Spirit lead
me on level ground. For your name's
sake, O LORD, preserve my life; in your
righteousness, bring me out of trouble.

Psalm 143:7-11

A Great Distress

O Lord,
Great distress has come upon me;
my cares threaten to crush me,
and I do not know what to do.
O God, be gracious to me and help me.
Give me strength to bear what You send,
and do not let fear rule over me …
Whether I live or die,
I am with You,
and You, My God, are with me.
Lord, I wait for Your salvation
and for Your kingdom.
Amen

∽ Dietrich Bonhoeffer ∽

Troubles Without Number

Do not withhold your mercy
    from me, O LORD;
  may your love and your
    truth always protect me.
For troubles without number
    surround me;
  my sins have overtaken me,
    and I cannot see.
They are more than the hairs of
    my head,
  and my heart fails within me.
Be pleased, O LORD, to save me;
  O LORD, come quickly to help me.

~ Psalm 40:11-13 ~

Strength for Daily Living

Give us, O God,
the power to go on,
To carry our share
of Thy burden through to the end,
To live all the years of our life
Faithful to the highest we have seen,
With no pandering to the second best,
No leniency to our own lower selves;
No looking backward,
No cowardice.
Give us the power to give ourselves,
To break the bread of our lives
unto starving humanity;
In humble self-subjection to serve others,
As Thou, O God, does serve Thy world.
Amen

J. S. Hoyland

Prayer for Favor

O Lord, God of heaven, the great and awesome God, who keeps his covenant of love with those who love him and obey his commands, let your ear be attentive and your eyes open to hear the prayer your servant is praying before you day and night for your servants, the people of Israel.

I confess the sins we Israelites, including myself and my father's house, have committed against you. O Lord, let your ear be attentive to the prayer of this your servant and to the prayer of your servants who delight in revering your name. Give your servant success today by granting him favor in the presence of this man.

Nehemiah 1:5-6, 11

Help in the Lord

In me there is darkness,
but with You there is light;
I am lonely, but You do not leave me;
I am feeble in heart,
but with You there is help;
I am restless, but with You there is peace.
In me there is bitterness,
but with You there is patience;
I do not understand Your ways,
but You know the way for me.
Lord Jesus Christ,
You were poor and in distress,
A captive and forsaken as I am.
You know all man's troubles;
You abide with me when all men fail me;
You remember and seek me;
It is Your will that I should know You
and turn to You.
Lord, I hear Your call and follow;
Help me.

∾ *Dietrich Bonhoeffer* ∾

Encouragement

May our Lord Jesus Christ himself
and God our Father,
who loved us
and by his grace
gave us eternal encouragement
and good hope,
encourage your hearts
and strengthen you
in every good deed and word.
~ 2 Thessalonians 2:16-17 ~

A Prayer at Bedtime

Blessed Creator,
Thou hast promised Thy beloved sleep;
Give me restoring rest
needful for tomorrow's toil.
If dreams be mine,
let them not be tinged with evil.
Let Thy Spirit make my time of repose
a blessed temple of His holy presence.
Withhold not Thy mercies
in the night season;
Thy hand never wearies,
Thy power needs no repose,
Thine eye never sleeps.

Help me when I helpless lie,
when my conscience accuses me of sin,
when my mind is harassed
by foreboding thoughts,
when my eyes are held awake
by personal anxieties.
Show Thyself to me as the God of all
grace, love, and power;
Thou hast a balm for every wound,
a solace for all anguish,
a remedy for every pain,
a peace for all disquietude.

Puritan Prayer

A Cry of Despair

How long, O Lord? Will you
forget me forever?
How long will you hide your
face from me?
How long must I wrestle with
my thoughts
and every day have sorrow in
my heart?
How long will my enemy
triumph over me?

Psalm 13:1-2

When the Load
is Too Heavy to Bear

Take Thou the burden, Lord;
I am exhausted with this heavy load.
My tired hands tremble,
and I stumble, stumble
along the way.
Oh, lead with Thine unfailing arm
again today.
Unless Thou lead me, Lord,
the road I journey is all too hard.
Through trust in Thee alone can I go on.
Yet not for self alone
thus do I groan;
My people's sorrows are the loads I bear.
Lord, hear my prayer –
may Thy strong hand
strike off all chains
that load my well-loved land.
God, draw her close to Thee.

Toyohiko Kagawa

An Infinite Resource

Almighty God, we respond to Thee in many different ways. Whatever our attitude, Father in heaven, rarely do we think of Thee as practical or relevant to our personal or corporate problems. Help us to understand that Thou art a God who cares – who seeks us – who longs for us. Help us see that Thou art the source of all wisdom and power – that Thou art an infinite resource available to meet our needs.

Forgive our indifference and grant us grace to call upon Thee however great or small our problems. Help us to see in the cross the measure of Your love, Your nearness, Your availability. In the name of Him whose mission was that of a sacrificial servant.

                    Richard Halverson

For Daily Tasks

O God,
Thou art with me
and it is Thy will
that these outward tasks
are given me to do.
Therefore I ask Thee, assist me,
and through it all
let me continue in Thy presence.
Be with me in this my endeavor,
accept the labor of my hands,
fill my heart as always.

— Brother Lawrence —

To Finish the Work

Grant, O merciful God,
that with malice toward none,
with charity for all,
with firmness in the right
as You give us to see the right,
we may strive to finish
the work we are in;
to bind up the nations' wounds …
to do all which may achieve
and cherish a just and lasting peace
among ourselves
and with all nations
through Jesus Christ our Lord.

◦ Abraham Lincoln ◦

For Strength

God give me strength.
Please get me through this.
Let me be the very best
I can be under these pressures.
Give me the power
and then I'm outta here.

— Bruce Jenner —

Petition

Understanding God

Gracious and holy Father,
give me wisdom to perceive You;
intelligence to fathom You;
patience to wait for You;
eyes to behold You;
a heart to meditate upon You;
and a life to proclaim You,
through the power
of the Spirit of Jesus Christ, our Lord.

⌒ Benedict ⌒

Gifts for the Daily Task

These are the gifts I ask
of Thee, Spirit serene:
Strength for the daily task,
courage to face the road,
good cheer to help me
bear the traveler's load,
and, for the hours that come between,
an inward joy
in all things heard and seen.
These are the sins I fain
would have Thee take away:
Malice, and cold disdain,
hot anger, sullen hate,
scorn of the lowly, envy of the great,
and discontent that casts a shadow gray
on all the brightness of the common day.

⌒ Henry van Dyke ⌒

Petition

When the weary, seeking rest,
to Thy goodness flee;
When the heavy-laden cast
all their load on Thee;
When the troubled, seeking peace,
on Thy name shall call;
When the sinner, seeking life,
at Thy feet shall fall:
Hear then in love, O Lord the cry,
in Heaven, Thy dwelling place on high.

⬧ John Greenleaf Whittier ⬧

Make Our Lives Count

Father, bless to our hearts
this word from Your Word.
Help us to make
our lives count for You.
Help us to serve You
with the strength of youth
… and the strength of age.
And take us at last into Your presence,
Through Jesus Christ our Lord.

Louis Benes

God Give Us Heroes

God give us heroes!
A time like this demands
strong minds, great hearts,
true faith and ready hands;
Those whom the lust
of office does not kill;
Those whom the spoils
of office cannot buy;
Those who possess
opinions and a will;
Those who have honor –
those who will not lie;
Those who can stand
before a demagogue
and damn his treacherous
flatteries without winking;

Petition

Tall folks, sun-crowned,
who live above the fog
in public duty
and in private thinking;
For while the rabble,
with their thumb-worn creeds,
their large professions
and their little deeds,
mingle in selfish strife, lo!
Freedom weeps,
wrong rules the land
and waiting Justice sleeps.

Josiah Holland

Supplication

Give me a good digestion, Lord,
And also something to digest;
Give me a healthy body, Lord,
With sense to keep it at its best.
Give me a healthy mind, good Lord,
To keep the good and pure in sight,
Which seeing sin is not appalled
But seeks a way to set it right.
Give me a mind that is not bored,
That does not whimper, whine, or sigh;
Don't let me worry overmuch
About the fussy thing called I.
Give me a sense of humor, Lord,
Give me the grace to see a joke,
To get some happiness from life
And pass it on to other folk.

Unknown

Let us then
approach the throne of grace
with confidence,
so that we may receive
mercy and find grace
to help us
in our time of need.
Hebrews 4:16